"When I confess that I often had to pause and catch my breath while reading *Two Open Doors in a Field*, I need you to know that such light-headedness was born of utter amazement and admiration. Sophie Klahr's poems are perpetual motion machines, stunning in all the ways they blaze through landscapes of adoration and epiphany and ache. From intimate sonnets to panoramic lyric sequences, from Jurassic seas to the spectral glow of motel pools and 'pulses of song' beneath a 'dark bowl of stars,' this synaptic second collection carries us across 'deep time' and its thresholds. She writes 'We must be / quiet to hear the universe. Must be attentive, then, must be very lucky,' and we are indeed blessed to lose ourselves with her in every astonishing turn, every luminous image."

—R. A. VILLANUEVA

"*Two Open Doors in a Field* is a road map for those of us needing to connect to the world around us, particularly in an era when we've felt so isolated from human connection. Like the Virgil of this journey, Terence, Klahr, too, finds nothing human foreign to her, and the journey welcomes both the public and the clandestine of the human condition. Rendered not only through a windshield view of what's possible up ahead but also of a relationship in the rearview mirror, formally nimble sonnets see the world clearly, and hold in the collection's core the long sequence 'Like Nebraska,' which, in its self-made form, offers both an elegant and an urgent simile for love. The road is long, the night wears on, but we have 'a place to sleep in her hands,' and Klahr 'makes a song from that' alone."

—A. VAN JORDAN

The
Backwaters
Press

The Backwaters Prize in Poetry
Honorable Mention

TWO OPEN DOORS IN A FIELD

Sophie Klahr

THE BACKWATERS PRESS | *An imprint of the University of Nebraska Press*

Acknowledgments for the use of copyrighted material appear on pages 73–77, which constitute an extension of the copyright page. All rights reserved. The Backwaters Press is an imprint of the University of Nebraska Press.

∞

Library of Congress Cataloging-in-Publication Data
Names: Klahr, Sophie, author.
Title: Two open doors in a field / Sophie Klahr.
Description: Lincoln: The Backwaters Press, an imprint of the University of Nebraska Press, [2023] | Series: The Backwaters prize in poetry honorable mention
Identifiers: LCCN 2022015051
ISBN 9781496232373 (paperback)
ISBN 9781496234834 (epub)
ISBN 9781496234841 (pdf)
Subjects: LCGFT: Poetry.
Classification: LCC PS3611.L345 T86 2023 | DDC 811/.6—dc23
LC record available at https://lccn.loc.gov/2022015051

Set in Garamond Premier Pro.

MAP

TWO OPEN DOORS IN A FIELD

I will go to the bank by the wood
and become undisguised . . .

—Walt Whitman, "Song of Myself"

Dawn on 101.5, The Fever:
Sometimes you're gonna have to lose, it sings.
Mice behind the lath, swallows in the eaves;
a rush of bergamot, wild sage drying
on the sill, boots already wet from dew.
The branches of a huge burn pile lift like
still-submerged coral. That old dream again:
the dream again   of the house that isn't.
Why don't you admit, you said, *that all roads
     lead to Nebraska*. In the time we spent
together, somewhere, a few languages
died. When you said   *It will always be un-
     even between us*, I heard a new word
for a field   impossible to measure

you explained something to me about fire
which I knew   I would quickly forget. *love
     is so short, forgetting is   so long.* this
had been something I needed, what you said

about the fire.   for weeks we touched only
          in the dark, pulsed like sea anemones.
every morning, you designed a new way
to leave. soon we lost an hour of daylight;

a turn signal of mine had broken—left
side, back.   I wanted to believe   I could
     fix it myself. winter had rolled onto
the acreage like someone turning in

bed, their palm smoothing to fit a lover's
rib.   when it snows, a car can disappear.

I followed a cloud
for three years
of my life I fell

—Frank Stanford

MOTEL, WYOMING

A kid in the parking lot asks me if
I live here—this is that kind of motel:
barren vending machine beneath the stairs,
a clock radio left on in the dark

when I first entered the room, little mess-
    ages noting what is broken, what not
to lean on. *Tonight I live here*, I say.
The Quiet Inn rests on the highway's lip.

So desperation is a part of what
a prophet must have. A minor prophet.
The best a prophet has is a question
no one really needs to know. We must be

quiet to hear the universe. Must be
attentive, then, must be very lucky.

I pulled over—the Jurassic sea was
spread in strata far across the canyon—
and sent a photograph of it to him.
I told him: *This was once a sea. As were
you*, he said. *There's no way for faith to be
a rock*, the Vatican astronomer
laughs, *why would I ever want such a thing?*
Just atom, just animal, symmetry;
Everything dies and that's how it should be,
isn't it? Too early gone, or too long
suffering—it's what we claim loss to be,
but even *Loss* is the wrong word. For what
is there, is, and what is not, we still live
with. The astronomer's laugh. What a life.

   and thinking of how in the ocean once,
waist-deep, we fought. I had started drinking
again, trying to stop. Was that the time
we stayed in a motel called The Sunrise?
White wicker, the peach-brushed walls, a prism
tied by fishing line to the fan so that
a jewel seemed to float midair? What year
was that was that the year he wrote *I can't*
be what grounds you? A song is slipping in—
  If you fall asleep down by the water—
Recall's accumulation swallows place.
(Or, tell it this way:) memory rips me
from the land. I miss an exit. I mis-
take this state for another. Take the wheel.

Another story. The murmuration
sweeps as a single form, a hungry wind
embodied over the cold riverbank—
the starlings—night falling without a place
to set camp.   *If you don't believe in ghosts,*
I said, *your loss.*   Lights of a town taken
for the hills on fire, penetrated air
mistaken for the scent of restless sleep
a poor triptych of orchids hung above.
The story of how gambling becomes ad-
        diction—loss-rush—one more night at The Red
Garter or Clearwater—familiar as
leaning bent against the pilled white bedspread,
my mouth saying *Hit me. Hit me again.*

MOTEL, OREGON

we'd rent the coastal room in an attempt
to say goodbye again as if   eros-
   ion could help us to undo what we had
done   again   we'd try to craft an ending

   eat cheap potato chips and Mountain Dew
the way he did the year his mother died
cradling herself   and the sound pushed him off-
shore . . . each room   strangulation and harbor

   we tried   *one day I'll leave not you but all*
this: those rooms that had never been under
my name   the way I could run my hand in
    longing to conjure a body I knew

so well I thought it home. *where o?* we left
all that   we made our bed   and lied in it

Watching Greek tragedies, unspeakable
violence makes us feel unearthed together—
in this version, a woman has been cast
as the hero, whose cries are so stripping
that her comrades abandon her, then real-
    ize they cannot win the war without her.
In the ancient world too, the play was per-
    formed by veterans for veterans. This
violence makes us feel at home together,
these miles 'til Bend, a needle threading blue
within the tall pines—a stitched horizon.
The disappearing hem of sky. Trauma
is never clean. Thunder begins. Then snow.
The story lost to static in the woods.

PARKED, CALIFORNIA

before a child is born an angel tells / them everything all the secrets of the / universe   &
then kisses them on the / forehead & they are born & they begin /   to forget.   this
stubbornly persistent / illusion: time as an arrow; *you were / born* goes the song and in that,
the child is / there. music can be like that: wrought timeless. / proverbs help us to remember
our grief / is not unique. I eat a bag of chips, / parked in a strip mall's lot, and meet the eyes
/ of someone else, parked. eating. three mirrors / to watch the night in. lower your eyes. now
/ listen.

you were born into a strange world

A fissure in the system: migration
too late this year, the water too warm, and
the seals must swim and swim much farther out
to hunt, their pups left too long on the shore.
Mothers return heavy with milk to find
pups laid limp on the rocks like thin dark burns,
and some mothers do not return at all.
There is always a turn, a last exit;
Las Vegas is sickly in the daylight—
I hold my body at the wheel as if
passing a graveyard, pulled by the tigers
and magic and women, endless buffets
straddling billboards; the suicide's blink.
Something is starving. Something holds its breath.

Suboxone: illusory, nomadic,
practical; the lighter with a sunset
on the ledge, the roominess of midnights
in small towns nodding out—all this, I like.
The cigarette stubbed twice on the rearview
mirror—this too I like. The little things:
cars lined up at seven a.m. before
the gate to see the meteor crater
has opened. Ruins of a Shell station.
The stand set up along a feeder road,
a hand-painted sign selling apricots.
I like the boy with his head in his hands.
In Russian, there are two words for the verb
Die. One for animals, one for people.

Clouds like braille like cures above the mesa.
A train cuts through the landscape, promising.
The girl ambles outside the bodega
holding her sentence: a hand-painted sign—
    I stole from this store—checks her reflection
in the window, runs a hand through her hair,
clear as an easy wink. Human shame is
so undependable; not believing
is perhaps a so much greater power
than belief. Simple to name this turning
as denial, but what if it is more
simple than even that? Shame is an o-
    pening, unbidden pining, a closed pin.
She drank the milk she stole, and slaked her thirst.

DRIVING THROUGH COLORADO, LISTENING TO THE RADIO

The forest has been waiting just for you!
says the radio   The radio says
Sparrow have you been practicing your song
Squirrel are you ready to really have fun
River how are your waters?   Come on in!
says the cartoon River, drained of itself—
Isn't it strange   how a highway can starve
     a town   and some people will think it's more
beautiful that way   (yes you   Silver Plume
Warm sunken beds of The Windsor Hotel
A museum made from your dead school   The gone
     tea room whose pleasant talk I swam in once
The wolf I saw   at your edge as a child
How each time I come back   looking for her—

Whale-song seeps against the mountains, backlit
with glimpses of cliff, bright inside the pines.
No one knew for years the sea contained sound,
but imagine the first who understood
those unfurling lengths as pulses of song,
imagine the first scientist who sighed
    My god, they're singing. And you too would have
gone *Oh my god,* whatever you believe.
It's just what happens when there's nothing else
to say. The memory of my father
standing in the snow, the blinding light not
of the sun but of his profile, sun-cut—
the way, atop the mountain, he would turn
and we'd follow, no matter what happened.

DRIVING THROUGH COLORADO, LISTENING TO THE RADIO, THINKING OF MY FATHER AGAIN

Oh yes, the radio says, *I notice*
when I feel God tapping me on the heart.
My father's story of a hitchhiker:
the young guy in a soldier's uniform
he picked up—the drive laden with hours left,
and the kid nice enough, hoping to reach
his girlfriend, he said, just in the next town.
Well look, the radio says, *God has wired*
our hearts for people.   *That's why I keep this*,
the kid had said, tugging his pant leg to
reveal the long hunting knife in his boot.
My father had asked him if he ever
felt afraid, entering a stranger's car.
I'm not a soldier either, said the kid.

Burrs, creeks, elms. . . . Here are some more things I like:
    the words *antidote* and *thistle*. Embers.
Each blown-out and pillaged motel along
state roads. How someone in a parking lot
asks how much I want for the cardboard globe
in my passenger seat. *The world*, I say.
How it seems the town where a young man was
crucified all those years ago became
gentle. The idea of deep time is
that we keep nothing, it just is what it
is. *It is what it is*—this too I like.
The friar's idea of The One Sadness.
God shed America—the boy being
dragged, naked: his body all our bodies.

DUST STORM

I dreamt I kissed your mouth
and felt the hours
trembling in my hair.

LIKE NEBRASKA

~

She leans like a ladder
Laid in the grass, thought
Lost for a season, now
Propped at the window to watch
A dust-colored horse
    with a white mane
Graze in a close paddock.
The horse is so close that when
Her heart goes out to it,
She can almost feel something
    coming back.
Tonight, no one else is staying here,
The motel pool still and blue as a pill.
Late at the desk tonight,
The receptionist tidies
A few faded leaflets
Like cars streaming by
On the freeway. At dawn,
The mountains beyond seem
Like an engine of light.
And beyond them, Nebraska.

~

He sleeps like an amber thread
Pulled through a sheet
Of shallow water, minnows flashing
Like half-memories
Risen while paused on a dirt road
To regard the dark bowl of stars
Hung over the grid of fields.
For an architect, it's easy
To get lost in Nebraska,
To simply turn
    towards the seed of loss.
If he turns
In bed towards the windows,
The seed can fly out each morning
To meet the slow shift of horizon
Becoming visible.
Nails hum in the burn pile.
That old dream again.

~

She listens like a horse
Patiently broken in
By the Good Lord himself.
There is no softer way.
In each scar, a story—
Pale comma of a slipped saw,
A welding spark.
In fields left unrazed for crops,
The grasshoppers part in waves
Where anyone walks.
Easy talk among the workers:
Irrigation bled into a wet spring,
Low ground now a stream
Ripe with frog-song.
The farmer is mowing a path
In what has gone
To seed. A body seen
Hovering among the goldenrod.

~

He speaks like a slow evening,
Some deep warm and nowhere-to-be.
She is memorizing his words—
    threshold, cairn, conduit, kiln—his lilt.
After the storm, the woodpile is wet, and
They break apart a splintered ladder
From beneath a stairwell to burn.
Horns of the drowsy steer downhill
Glint like a pistol tucked into a stranger's belt.
Faults in the drywall, in the banister; black mold
Along the foundation in the farmhouse. A myth
The workers whisper: how beneath
The house someone's shovel once found
An apothecary bottle, a woman's glove, a shoe
Preserved in that soft dry dirt.

~

She rustles like a stream
Found swollen wider at daybreak;
Lightning scurried all night,
Hailstones grazing each vein
In the dead cottonwood—
There is too much want
        to name.
She moves along the line
Wringing out wet clothing
To hang again.
Crickets tuning, catnip
Kissing henbit, yellow flash
Of the woodpecker's underwing—
Suppose you can get
        what you want

~

He stands like a sailor,
Two-days-sweat
In the small of his back.
From the roof, he sees
Where she has crouched
    in a far field
To read the bed
Deer pressed last night,
Chin cupped in one hand
Like a tired childhood,
A monarch asleep
    on the milkweed.
Two birds dissect the heat wave—
Gold filaments of call.
He sees her rise
    towards the bordering trees,
Lifting her shirt,
Knotting the tails.
He tightens his belt
Like a shoreline.

~

She prays like a pure habit
    of curiosity: magnifying
Glass to an anthill, legs split
From daddy longlegs,
A live cicada tied to a string
    and so on.
Prayer is simply what comes
As she works alone to build
A dike the farm needs to stay afloat.
Every few thrusts into the soil,
    she thinks, *god* . . .
Sometimes a question enters
The word like a burr, a seed
With a hundred hooks for arms.
None of the old tunes feel right.
She goes out to an edge of a field
Where many things are rusted,
Finds a perch on a sinking thresher
    embedded with brush.
Remembers she always has
A place to sleep in her hands.
Makes a song from that.

~

He moves like leading lights—
    one onshore, one off—
Which once aligned, show ships
Either how to come to harbor or how
To leave. There is clockwork
To a fire, how long to crouch
Exhaling hard before
The logs will catch.
He tells her to say *White rabbit*
Three times: a spell to keep
From swallowing smoke.
One worker is homesick, singing
    Don't mistake your guide
      for what you're looking for,
And the song is about Orion too,
    and bitten rooms, and thunder . . .
When their friend goes quiet, they can hear
Paths moving outside the fire's edge,
Little bluestems bending, raccoons
Out there in the dark, cupping
Each so-human hand to their hungers.

~

She pauses like a mare
Losing a foal,
And the mare doesn't have
The word *Death*, or any words.
A spider lands on her chest,
Sure-footed, pure as a barn hex.
She brushes it back towards the sun,
    away from where she's been
Fixing a rotting window frame.
One failure, then another—
    nails lost in the soft wood.
Outside, the sound of some machine—
The farmer's hands
Putting something back together
Or cutting something new.

~

He draws like a lighthouse
Holds itself: set in a landscape
Made to beckon another—
One has to climb inside
    for a chance
To feel the gravity of that.
Each day, he digs the beginning
Of something like a well,
Which he now sees as an eye,
The base of one well
Knit by a bricked tunnel
To another just wide enough
    to lie down in.
Then, one could look up
And through an open flue, see
That dark spot at the center
    of anybody's iris.
He is building something
The farm doesn't need;
Wind runs to examine
The new organ
In the southern field.
It's late—he's drawing in
What soon he'll be
Unable to undo, the way
One cannot undo having placed a finger
In someone else's mouth.

~

She writes like a trail
Come upon in the morning mud,
Tracks large enough to give
Anyone pause—they say
You don't know
What you're living with,
Or where it sleeps.

~

He unfolds like a lunar eclipse—
A stammer at the clearing's edge
He's been watching while he smokes,
Convinced it is an animal
But when the light shifts, it is not.
Steam from the shower sets
Like fog in the sleeping house,
Faint ochre of brick dust
Snaking in the water—
A color he'd mistaken for his skin.
Any eclipse takes a while.
One body shadowing another.
He clears vapor from the mirror
To look himself in the eye,
        like the dead shrew's incisors
When a flashlight caught them—

~

She shifts like the word *caliper*,
Its echo the sound of a stallion
Tearing through a field. He says *caliper*,
To answer her question, bending
His bare wrist up from his work glove
To brush   sweat
        from his eye.
She presses the third beat of the word
From the roof of her mouth
        to her lips: *caliper, caliper . . .*
On the east side of the acreage,
Two new workers build an oven,
Speak of pickling okra with
An oak leaf and peppercorns,
Draw a map of the once-buried garden.
Caliper, she thinks, and looks at the tools
Scattered in the grass, their weight,
And how he translates them.
Now he is saying something
To do with sightlines. A cipher.
Offering her a cigarette.
His sleeve brushing hers.

~

He fades like the white animal
Glimpsed only once
In the wild rye and gone,
His customary turning like a sky
That looks like rain but does not rain.
It is mosquito hour, thin songs
Visiting each body like a violin's
Sharp lift at the end of a story—
The air is full of strings.
There is dirt in his cut knuckle,
Cheap beer on the table,
The kitchen lit by a single bulb
And workers laughing how and where
They'll go when harvest ends.
I am going to sleep, he says,
Crushes his cans and climbs in the dark
Back to the barn's forecastle, to his bed
Where the walls seem to luff in the wind.

~

She reels like a cradle
Made of a wide dirt road
    and two fields of corn
The road rides between;
Landscape-reaching-never-touching,
Fields watching one another;
A type of vertigo, seeing
    all that sky.
Her arm out the passenger's window,
Wind-braced, fingertips
Skimming the height of the crops.
Again heat-dumb, they slip away
Together to the quarry, and again, damp,
Slip back into his car the color of sky
A child would choose for a sky.
Something is dead in the road,
Open to whatever after life might be.
Each time they pass, the dashed body
More itself than what it had been.
Her hand at the nape of his neck
Until he shifts, imperceptibly, away.

~

He wanders like a record
Skips—an idea
With a dropped stitch.
The belly of the barn yawns
Like a ship's hold in the dim light
Let in by the open door. He is
Searching for a tool the farmer's
Waved him towards, remembering
The squirrel he shot once,
How it fell
More like a bird.
After September, he has
No plans.
Each day he thinks
He'll make a plan.
Almost the end now of September.
A train comes through the county
Only at night or at least
He hears it only at night.
Flying ants have come
To the kitchen this morning.
They stream upwards
On the windows
Like wrong black rain.

~

She wakes like a crow
Landing in a dry pasture—
The cattle only lift their eyes.
A surprise, to have slept so long:
Boots still tied,
A catnap from the heat
Rolled into dusk.
Caught between screen and pane,
A moth berates itself
Like a nervous thief.
Insect singing thickens
After sunset, cut grass
Laid in heaps still
Intimate with the uncut grass.
The scent of roasting sausages
Drapes itself along a stairwell.
Somewhere tomorrow
        is her crowbar, lath waiting
To be torn.
Miles away, in town,
A woman is calling out
From a porch light's edge,
Waiting for her boys to come home.

~

He drinks like the faithful,
    the way they fold their hands
In church, like two owls roosting in an elm.
Karaoke night at the Don't Care Bar:
A worker staggers, following the lyric
To a lit-up song, and outside,
A stranger chews their ears off
About *the Green Desert*: fields of soy and corn
And soy and corn and soy,
Devoid of flowers, *and the bees going damn drunk*
    with hunger.
She leans into him like a stray cat against a fence.
A hundred species of insects, the stranger tells them, *in a space*
    where there should have been a thousand.
A truck leaving backfires.
Beneath the only streetlight, a possum
Practices its death.
His hand at the small of her back,
On the depthless roses painted
On her old black dress.

~

She hopes like a root—
Bare instinct, without pleasure
    or absence of pleasure.
Once it reaches the field,
The water's hand
Falls asleep—no frog-song
    in the runoff.
Two ponies, shades of birch
And chestnut, nuzzle one another
Softly in agreement:
Amen, amen.
She is a part of the moth
And the word *moth* in his mouth;
A town named after a type of bruise,
Town named for an island no island.
His coming to her door
Like a blue quilt cast over a bed,
In the air that simply, coming to rest.

~

He sighs like a hinge in an empty cabin
Found by a traveler smelling of fire.
Are you still you? he murmurs,
And lying beside him,
She can't say.
She's found the jade dress
In a barrel of clothing
Past workers abandoned.
Torn in the arm,
In the belly by a nail,
And either
She'll patch the holes
Or she won't.
He's told her
How a clutch of baby mice
Fell from the rafters of this room—
    the highest point for miles—
Nails in the eaves melted
Flat from past lightning.
The mice still harboring
Their blushed shadow of birth.
How he opened the door to the roof
    and swept their bodies like petals
With a straw broom into the dark.
He puts his hand under the dress.
You are many different landscapes, he says.

~

She feels like the warm springs
Of a screen door pushed open quickly
And knocking back once in its frame to rest.
From a distance, the gray in his hair glints
Like mica in the sun.
Their distance swells like a bite.
She thinks of excuses to cross the field—
To ask for a nail, for a match.
Her daydream goes like this: she lifts
Her palm to his cheek.
He looks at her
And puts his mouth to her palm.

~

He rises like a gamble taken
In the afterlight of a fire
Chanced with damp wood:
What burned despite itself.
From the gamble stems
Other questions like maple seeds,
Which opened, lift
    into the air . . .
What does it mean, anyway,
To meet someone.
Regret and not quite regret,
The houses asleep, someone
Dreaming of a poisoned dog.
He is walking past the truck
Heavy with a bed of sand
Workers pulled from the river;
He is walking into the fog,
    into the dew at dawn.
What does it mean
    to meet someone anyway

~

She sways like a house in strong wind,
Loves how the house sways
    in strong wind
Like watching him walk from far away
Back home through the fields, love
Being just some constellation you can gaze at
For so long you think it is moving

    Like a house in the wind

Or a man in a field

~

He digs like a grasshopper sings—
    to recall something.
Points the auger to carve
Where he wants the hole to dwell,
Grips the long handle and jumps
His weight onto the shovel.
Flickering silver: the shovel's palm.
Only his profile visible
Some moments in the tallgrass;
It seems, the way the shovel flies,
    he might be
Slaughtering something.
A scrap of blue cloth tied to a post
Marks where he wants
Another shape to open:
A steady eye at a window.
He watches her
Wind across the meadow
To see how deeply he's dug so far—
The deepest point
Drifts at his ribs.
It is a machine, he explains,
    for remembering.

~

She breathes like a river
At the first melt of winter
And thinks of the blood moon
Approaching, how it will pass
Through earth's shadow.
Her body stretches along
The north barn's roof,
An angle risked to pull
Nails from a rotting toeboard.
Below, within, a worker paints a mask:
The face of a creature
Whose feet turn the wrong way,
So when it runs, only
Its past can be followed.
She steadies her hip
On a shingle.
The worker is lifting
The mask to her face.

~

He comes like a fox—
Quick run of heat in the dark
    places his hands on
Each side of her head
As if to absolve.   As if
They were both treading water.
At dawn, a strange bee alights
On the collar of her dress
Just as she slips it over her head.
That's not fair, he hears her say
    to the bee.
In the field,
The hole is deep enough now
That he must hoist himself out
Like a swimmer's careful pressing
    up against the lip of a rock.
Earth, his book says,
    is the most forgiving element.

~

She sees like a memory aware of itself as memory;
He is dressing in the half-dark like some old movie:
A man in a dream of farmland, his profile
    plucked from switchgrass, made visible
By light casting its line inwards,
His pale body smelling of flight like a familiar story.
An entire landscape curving to pull on a pair of boots.

~

They are like Nebraska
At the end of September:
Still-blooming marigolds heaped
In the garden, a familiar quilt
    being unfolded; cold at sunrise
Easy in the air and water stains
Like veins below a window sill,
Coffee cup beside the feather bed;
A memory of cottonwood drifts,
Tall nodding phlox, brick dust
    again in his hair.
Rose hips wild in a ditch,
A cricket singing *Keep it, Keep it*
    from behind the leaking washer.
Dust lit by shafts of sun
Streaming through cracks
In the north barn's roof,
Light resting on shoulders
Worn out with the good work
    of a good day.
The closest town to the farm
Named simply
For the first who decided to stay.
This is how September ends—
They stand together at dusk,
A little ways apart,
Like two open doors
In a field

CODA: THE HOLE I DUG

I watched a robin
standing vigil

at her torn storm
-downed nest

Saw her seeing
her dead chicks

I had watched
the eggs hatch

I had been
some small part

of the land each day and now
stood at the distance

I'd always been—
See

a hawk, a fox
at dawn

a bite, a burn
an aperture—

Am I writing
about the land

or the shape
the eye makes

of the land?
Trodden acres—

my looking—
Without this land,

what will we have
to say   How

will we speak
to one another

Following the shore
I choose the long way home

— Frank Stanford,
"Memory Is Like a Shotgun . . ."

DRIVING THROUGH CALIFORNIA, LISTENING TO THE RADIO

The clerk with Chinese characters running
down his arm at the gas station's counter,
one cheekbone dusted with acne as if
he'd turned his face   to listen to something
like a high whine in the fiberglass wind . . .
"Christian Answers Live" in the still-dark dawn:
        If He knows what we're gonna do before
we're born, why make us if we're going to
hell?   *I get questions like this every day,*
the pastor says, *and I'm obligated*
as a human being to seek. I'm not
going to tell you anything you don't
already know. The clerk's whiteness twitches.
Remind me how God's promises translate.

Again, the interstate. A song about
Elvis, how *he shook it and it rang like*
silver. Hey, Horizon City. I swear,
this morning I saw the hands of God in
Phoenix, streaming over rush hour traffic.
We are supposed to be shook. I will change
what I can change, will try to leave the rest.
A billboard misread: "zip line adventures,"
not "opioid crisis." In my hometown
back east, the newspaper prints six pictures
of kids who have overdosed. I once knew
a few. We held hands and prayed for our lives,
or at least, we tried. White sneakers in church
basements. White sneakers at the funerals.

MOTEL, ARIZONA

Beyond two nights in any motel seems
to threaten moving on—again, morning
opens back a stiff plastic curtain to
the asphalt galaxy, the glittering

of a plot that swallows velocity.
I walk from the edge of town to a store
where vegetables shine and wince in my hands.
I say something nice to the young cashier,

return to the room. Turn to a letter.
Sometimes you just have to die about it,
writes my friend. She means *mourn*, in her broken
English. Animals only pace in zoos.

On TV, people are playing a game,
clapping when the holes in the world are named.

PARKED, UTAH

        & the sun begins to rise so quickly—
(*I've got nothing to hide*, she sings)—   salt flats

      in first light, a wing bone. Frostbit windows;
      the soft shoulder. 10 miles 'til Wendover.

        I pull over to the side of the road
thick with low sloped un-darkening salt brush,

    (*tell me what you want tell me what you want*)
      & your hand presses the nape of my neck

       & you're only someone I've imagined.
    Seeing a state's different with somebody.

      It was first written in animal blood:
    No harm shall come unto thee. Another

      bright idea. As long as there has been
    a truth to tell, there has been a liar.

Silhouette of a hoofed beast, dark branches
in profile again, amarillo frame.
Knife City, crosswinds; the memory of
dusting a table with his shirt; outlaw,
split cactus, sparrow hawk. Remembering
is so often an act of contrition.
I would not have chosen to find myself
here, ground to pieces, but nothing truly
human is abhorrent to me. I don't
know the lineage between deer and elk—
I know the signs warn me of their leaping,
like the risen memory of that shirt, un-
bidden. Then—what? I washed and hung it on
the line, open-armed. Mended what was torn.

PARKED, TEXAS

Yes—alone, I could stop for anything.
Fossil bed at a river's wrist.   Hello

aoudad on Blue Mountain, javelina
gnawing cactus, Stinky the cat hiding

in a closet. Every bee takes an hour
and that hour is the bee's. Vultures braid through

the sky against the mountain. I under-
stand now, how one could come to doubt words here.

I learn a few names of people to call
friends. We pause in the dark, silent, looking

towards a light at a distance no one can
figure out, our backs to a fading glyph.

The starved coyote in a rancher's trap
is shot. A type of rain bleeds from its mouth.

He dies in every living room in town
sings Johnny Cash. Feels like leaving Texas
takes forever. In the next town over
a cheap room is waiting on me. A sign:
    the natural choice is life. A small rose
with thorns painted childlike beneath. I am
reassured mine is a short life; many
beautiful ideas turn out to be
wrong. Humans are just waves of happenings,
and the more a distance is, the more ache
it has room to carry. Do you feel me?
In the mid-morning fog: another sign:
    abortion kills jesus forgives—and thus
I am forgiven. What an idea.

"Oh, What a Beautiful Mornin'" hidden
inside Beethoven's "Moonlight Sonata"—
the Piano Puzzler of the Day, solved
by the first caller. The sonata was
written for Julie, who did not love him.
All the sounds of the earth are like music—
Imagine if the moon felt such a thing.
Could one familiar song be home enough?
O the more a distance is the more ache
it has room to carry; fermata—*wait,
find me.*   Lizst had liked the middle movement,
called it "a flower between abysses."
You'll recognize this, says the radio.

DRIVING THROUGH KANSAS, LISTENING TO THE RADIO

I have only ever seen the shadow
of clouds on the ocean and on the plains.
As in   *your body / spilled on my body /*
seen / dissolved / makes the watching real.   A choir
on The River sings an arrangement of
"Amazing Grace," poultry like fall leaves sleep
outside the dim light of the auction's door,
and just like that—it's gone: another town
whose name I'll never try to remember.
I think before you came into my mouth
you were a fever   made of my watching—
a cloud-shape I could know but could not name,
like those walls printed with ash and honey—
a pattern I could track but could not touch.

HARVEST

Nebraska talked in its sleep in my mouth
      all winter   then spring

transcribing the fall before
      the spring again:

Compass plant and prairie blazing star
goldenrod and floating barn

each mile-long stretch of crops amid
the lettered roads

low bridge above
the swollen Platte

even the tangle we slept in
each season like an omen—that question

of what would that land have been to us
without the other—

It was real life after all

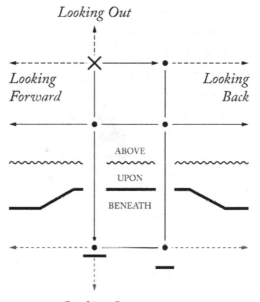

Looking Out

Looking
Forward

Looking
Back

ABOVE

UPON

BENEATH

Looking In

PASS WITH CARE

Pass with care says the road, says *do not pass*—
Every photograph I take of ruins
is with you in mind; agony, orchard,
gasoline, comfort; seeking some being
in these arced hours, no other cars mirage
to punctuate fences beyond fences,
long syllables of wires or their absence,
any living creatures beside cattle;
I but use you for a minute, then I
resign you, stallion—the CD skipping—
What / What / What is less or more than a touch—
a kind of marginalia to the land
that I listen to over and over;
can I say how empty this country seems

~

Can I say how empty this country seems?
Land razed; shocked fertility needing time
for its soul to catch up to its body,
and I am complicit. . . . There: horseheads of
pumpjacks nod bleak nods over the oil fields,
beaks heavy in the stripped miles; I struggle;
this country emptied by us and porous
and beloved and how I've neglected
the sky in what I have tried to tell you

let me tell you—by god, it was so blue.

The wind moves like an animal inside
the grass beyond my wheel. I don't know if
I understand how to see myself home
but I've gathered all these pieces to me

~

But I've gathered all these pieces to me
like bones that might have breath leaned back into
each length. On my dashboard: eucalyptus,
seashells, stones . . . ;   I do want to have a home.
It snowed in the town where I woke today
but I still haven't seen the rain in months
and the earth mutters on, holding itself,
erosion the origin of sweet talk.
I'd like to report: *I will put Chaos*
into fourteen lines. I'd like to report,
passing No Whiners Diner in Roswell
cattycorner from The Caverns Motel—
Can you hear me? I say into the phone.
How often this question means giving up

~

How often this question means giving up:
I ask a lover if they will write me
once I arrive in _____. *I won't,* they say,
that's just not the kind of person I am.
A woman is even more a woman
when she sleeps alone and even more so
in a bed not her own   (I think often
of being chopped into little pieces)
        I am weary with being a woman
so clearly a Woman   Woman seeing
America   white Jewish sober queer
Woman seeing America   O—I
met my five-year-old trans cousin last week—
He knew himself so well it made me weep

~

(He knew himself so well it made me weep
    or was it me that I was weeping for)

In the shade of a rest stop, a trucker
and I standing on the pavilion watch
as the fenced land it seems we have each been
staring into is split by a line of
    dogs.   After the fourth it no longer seems
like a dream—dogs glimpsed beyond the barbed wire
becoming fact.   The trucker wears a hat
bearing the name of who he believed would

make America Great Again. Seeing
the dogs, we turn to one another, strange
awe making us light. At least this we shared.
It's not something I would want to forget

~

It's not something I would want to forget—
I lift a wounded snake from a dirt road;
I have always loved believing I could
save things until the spring I trapped raccoons,

two kits, one hurt by being tangled in
tarp strings I spent all afternoon cutting
away from its body. Set the kits up
in a live trap for their mother's entry,

the point was to keep them a family . . .
Three nights she came to take them from the cage
A fault in the latch kept   shutting her out
    she tried—   (piss fur flesh ripped)   she left a trail . . .

It fills me with shame to say this, and still
it's a story I have to do justice

~

It's a story I have to do justice—
     there was a badger hole beside the house
I saw my hair woven into a nest
     behind the lath   a wind slammed the door hard
         then opened it   quiet as a mother
petals of an altar's yellow roses
like chiggers that lit up beneath my skin
     whenever I ran   The memory was that
of someone fleeing   I've not said I want
to be alone   I'd like a passenger
Perhaps you have become my passenger
by reading   my worn car's door flung open
and here   I will leave it open   for you.
Do not pass says the road   *Pass with care* the road says

GENERAL NOTE ON CREATION

Between 2015 and 2018 the author drove alone for approximately 14,452 miles on a variety of loops between Nebraska and California. Many initial notes were taken via voice recording; the bulk of this book is one of collaged listening, first drafted quite literally while driving. Due to this mode of creation, some poems may contain misremembered and/or unattributed quotes heard on the radio, though confirmation and correct citation have been thoroughly attempted with good efforts and intentions.

Particular Notes

DRIVING THROUGH NEBRASKA, LISTENING TO THE RADIO
includes lyrics from "The Climb" by Miley Cyrus, as well as an idea found in filmmaker Werner Herzog's book *Conquest of the Useless*.

PARKED, NEBRASKA
includes a line from Pablo Neruda's "Tonight I Can Write the Saddest Lines."

MOTEL, WYOMING
was informed by Krista Tippet's *On Being* interview with Walter Brueggemann.

DRIVING THROUGH UTAH, LISTENING TO THE RADIO
contains paraphrases from Krista Tippet's *On Being* interview with Father George Coyne and Brother Guy Consolmagno.

LISTENING TO THE RADIO, DRIVING THROUGH NEVADA AGAIN
includes lyrics from "Down by the Water" by the Drums.

DRIVING THROUGH OREGON, LISTENING TO THE RADIO
takes inspiration from an NPR story on Theater of War, an organization designed to help military personnel cope with the emotional toll of war through the reading of plays and facilitation of public discussion. This poem refers to Sophocles's play *Philoctetes*.

PARKED, CALIFORNIA

contains paraphrases from Krista Tippet's *On Being* interview with Craig Minowa of Cloud Cult, a quote from a letter of Albert Einstein's to a grieving friend, and lyrics from "You Were Born" by Cloud Cult.

DRIVING THROUGH WYOMING, LISTENING TO THE RADIO and LISTENING TO THE RADIO, DRIVING THROUGH NEW MEXICO AGAIN

both contain thoughts from Krista Tippet's *On Being* interview with Friar Richard Rohr. This includes Rohr paraphrasing the Latin poet Terance: "Nothing truly human is abhorrent to me." The former poem is written with the memory of Matthew Shepherd, murdered in 1988 in an anti-gay hate crime near Laramie, Wyoming.

LIKE NEBRASKA

was created while exclusively reading *What About This: Collected Poems of Frank Stanford*. The sequence, and much of this book, is indebted to Stanford. The quote "Don't mistake your guide for what you're looking for" is from my friend Faith Eliott's song "Insects."

LISTENING TO THE RADIO, DRIVING THROUGH ARIZONA AGAIN

contains lyrics from "Elvis Presley Blues" by Gillian Welch.

PARKED, UTAH

includes a twist of lyrics from "More Than" by Au Revoir Simone and quotes from John Leacock's biblical parodic satire *The First Book of the American Chronicles of the Times* and paraphrases Psalm 91:10–12 from the New King James Bible.

DRIVING THROUGH TEXAS, LISTENING TO THE RADIO and DRIVING THROUGH OKLAHOMA, LISTENING TO THE RADIO

both contain a line borrowed from my friend Ryan Paradiso ("the more a distance / to carry"). The former contains lyrics to "Out Among the Stars" by Johnny Cash and ideas from Krista Tippet's *On Being* interview with Carlo Rovelli. The latter includes lyrics from the 1943 Rodgers and Hammerstein musical *Oklahoma!*

DRIVING THROUGH KANSAS, LISTENING TO THE RADIO
borrows an idea from my friend the ceramicist Casey Whittier ("the shadow
/ of clouds . . ."), and contains lines from Octavio Paz's "A Draft
of Shadows."

HARVEST
contains a variation of Octavio Paz's line in "The River": "all night long the
city talks in its sleep through my mouth."

PASS WITH CARE
contains lines from Walt Whitman's "Song of Myself" and alludes to lyrics
from Joni Mitchell's album *Hejira*. "[I will put Chaos into fourteen lines]"
is a sonnet by Edna St. Vincent Millay.

ACKNOWLEDGMENTS

Great thanks to the readers and editors of these literary publications in which poems herein previously appeared:

AGNI

Alaska Quarterly Revie

Foglifter

Frontier Poetry

Gettysburg Review

Hobart

Interrupture

Los Angeles Review

Michigan Quarterly Review

Neck

Ploughshares

Poetry London

The Rumpus

Southern Indiana Review

Zócalo Public Square

ZYZZYVA

Excerpts from "Like Nebraska" appeared in *Alaska Quarterly Review*, *Bennington Review*, *Blackbird*, the *Cincinnati Review*, *Colorado Review*, the *New Yorker*, *Nomadic Ground*, *Poet Lore*, *Poetry Northwest*, and *Third Coast*, as well as in the anthology *Constant Stranger: After Frank Stanford*, edited by Max Crinnin and Aidan Ryan (Foundlings Press, 2018).

Looking Diagram (Fig. 1) is courtesy of Colin Chudyk.

GRATITUDES

Thank you to the Stadler Center for Poetry and Literary Arts and to the University of North Carolina for granting me the time to gather my thoughts. Love to all in The Rooms I frequent, who trudge the road of happy destiny. Love to those I danced with in Los Angeles (love to Meliss in particular). Deep thanks to Eileen Myles and Cass McCombs, who gave me shelter (and much more)—I will do my best to pay your kindness forward. Thanks to A. Van Jordan and to Brenda Hillman—our brief overlaps made all the difference. Thanks to Mark Doty for the warm and thoughtful eye.

Love to all residents who shared the acreage and its radius during my patchwork year and a quarter at Art Farm—thank you for digging and dismantling and cooking and building and gardening and sharing your lives with me. Particular gratitude to Casey Whittier, Faith Eliott, Jesse Gegenbach, Jessie Lipsett, Jules Jameson, Fiona Cashell, Rob Meeker, Nicole V. Basta, Ariel Yelen, and Laura "from Aurora" Rybeck—thank you for the goodness of your work and your hearts.

Love to my family of origin for your embrace of my strange life and for some of the gas money. Love to my cousin Bobbie for being a haven in the Southwest. Love to Gregory Barnett, Craig Bernier, Dorothy Hoover, Ryan Paradiso, Emma Rogers, Anna Seva, Matthew Siegel, Corey Zeller, and Anna Vogelzang for getting it / everything. Love to Ted Kooser for the wholly unexpected gift of your care and kinship—you are so much a part of my Nebraska.

Finally, thank you to the spirit of my car (Crystal, now crushed somewhere in West Virginia), which enabled me to see so much and was so often my only constant during the years I wrote this book, especially when I had no full-time home. Thanks to the duct-taped side mirror for sticking with me.

Dedication

This book is for Ed Dadey, generous visionary and Fearless Leader of Art Farm, who gave me a home, and for Colin Chudyk, who once gave me a compass. Where and what would I be or have been without you?

BACKWATERS PRIZE IN POETRY

2021   Laura Bylenok, *Living Room*
       Honorable Mention: Sophie Klahr, *Two Open Doors in a Field*
2020   Nathaniel Perry, *Long Rules: An Essay in Verse*
       Honorable Mention: Amy Haddad, *An Otherwise Healthy Woman*
2019   Jennifer K. Sweeney, *Foxlogic, Fireweed*
       Honorable Mention: Indigo Moor, *Everybody's Jonesin' for Something*
2018   John Sibley Williams, *Skin Memory*
2017   Benjamín Naka-Hasebe Kingsley, *Not Your Mama's Melting Pot*
2016   Mary Jo Thompson, *Stunt Heart*
2015   Kim Garcia, *DRONE*
2014   Katharine Whitcomb, *The Daughter's Almanac*
2013   Zeina Hashem Beck, *To Live in Autumn*
2012   Susan Elbe, *The Map of What Happened*
2004   Aaron Anstett, *No Accident*
2003   Michelle Gillett, *Blinding the Goldfinches*
2002   Ginny MacKenzie, *Skipstone*
2001   Susan Firer, *The Laugh We Make When We Fall*
2000   David Staudt, *The Gifts and the Thefts*
1999   Sally Allen McNall, *Rescue*
1998   Kevin Griffith, *Paradise Refunded*

The Backwaters Prize in Poetry was suspended from 2005 to 2011.

To order or obtain more information on these or other University of Nebraska Press titles, visit nebraskapress.unl.edu.

Printed in the USA
CPSIA information can be obtained
at www.ICGtesting.com
LVHW050735030224
770777LV00002B/141